HOW TO MAKE MONEY ONLINE AT HOME

ACHIEVING FULL-TIME INCOME, FROM POVERTY TO PROSPERITY, THROUGH STRATEGIC FINANCIAL GROWTH

copyright@2024

Danny crooms

TABLE OF CONTENT

CHAPTER 1: UNDERSTANDING THE ONLINE MARKETPLACE 12
CHAPTER 2: FREELANCING 21
    IDENTIFYING MARKETABLE SKILLS 21
CHAPTER 3: BLOGGING AND CONTENT CREATION 46
    CHOOSING A NICHE 46
CHAPTER FOUR: AFFILIATE MARKETING .. 62
    HOW AFFILIATE MARKETING WORKS .. 62
CHAPTER 5: E COMMERCE AND DROP SHIPPING 84
    SETTING UP AN ONLINE STORE (SHOPIFY, WOO COMMERCE) 84

INTRODUCTION

Welcome to "Making Money Online: Your Guide to Digital Success." In the age of virtual transformation, the net has spread out a myriad of opportunities for individuals to earn cash from the consolation of their personal houses. Whether you're seeking to complement your earnings, transition to a full time online profession, or surely discover new avenues for monetary growth, this e book is designed to guide you every step of the way.

PURPOSE OF THE BOOK

The primary purpose of this ebook is to offer a complete and realistic guide to making money online. We will delve into numerous strategies and techniques that have proven a hit for many people. From freelancing to e commerce, blogging to making an investment, this e book will cover a huge variety of opportunities to healthy distinct talents and interests.

OVERVIEW OF OPPORTUNITIES

The net is a significant and dynamic marketplace with severa opportunities to earn money. Some of the maximum popular and effective methods to make money on line consist of:

- Freelancing: Offering your competencies and offerings to clients around the sector.
- Blogging and Content Creation: Sharing treasured content material and monetizing your audience.
- Affiliate Marketing: Promoting products and incomes commissions.
- E commerce and Drop shipping: Selling merchandise thru on line stores.
- Online Courses and Coaching: Teaching and mentoring others.

- Investing and Trading: Growing your wealth through on line investment platforms.
- Remote Work and Virtual Assistance: Providing administrative and specialized guide remotely.
- Social Media and Influencer Marketing: Leveraging social media platforms to earn cash.
- YouTube and Video Content Creation: Creating engaging video content.
- Writing and Self Publishing: Publishing ebooks and written content.

WHO CAN BENEFIT

This ebook is for all people who desires to discover the capacity of getting cash on-line, irrespective of their historical past or enjoy degree. Whether you're a student looking for part time paintings, a stay a thome discern looking for flexible profits, a professional aiming to diversify your sales streams, or a retiree exploring new ventures, this manual is adapted that will help you attain your economic desires.

WHY MAKE MONEY ONLINE?

The appeal of creating wealth on-line lies in its flexibility, scalability, and accessibility.

- Flexibility: Work from anywhere, at any time, and set your personal time table.
- Low Startup Costs: Many on line ventures require minimal investment to get commenced.
- Global Reach: Access a global market of customers and customers.
- Diverse Opportunities: Choose from a wide range of fields and industries.
- Scalability: Grow your online enterprise at your very own tempo.

Getting Started

The adventure to being profitable on-line starts with a unmarried step. As you embark in this interesting course, remember that success requires dedication, perseverance, and a willingness to learn and adapt. The net is continuously evolving, and staying knowledgeable and flexible might be key for your long term achievement.

WHO CAN BENEFIT

The digital landscape offers possibilities for individuals from all walks of existence. This book is crafted to cater to a various audience, ensuring that anybody interested by being profitable on-line can find valuable steering and proposal. Let's discover who can gain from this complete guide:

STUDENTS

- Part Time Income: Students trying to earn cash without compromising their studies can discover bendy online jobs and freelance opportunities.
- Skill Development: Engaging in on line work lets in students to increase

marketable skills, benefit real world enjoy, and build a professional portfolio.
- Financial Independence: Earning cash online can offer students with monetary independence, lowering reliance on loans and parental aid.

STAY AT HOME PARENTS

- Work Life Balance: Stay a thome parents can locate online paintings that suits around their circle of relatives commitments, allowing them to contribute financially while being present for his or her youngsters.
- Flexible Schedule: Online opportunities frequently provide the flexibility to paintings during nap times, faculty hours, or evenings.
- Utilizing Existing Skills: Parents can leverage their existing capabilities in areas such as writing, picture design, or virtual help to earn cash from domestic.

PROFESSIONALS

- Diversified Income Streams: Professionals can supplement their number one income by using exploring on-line facet hustles or freelance gigs.
- Career Transition: Those seeking to transition to a new profession can use online possibilities to benefit enjoy and establish themselves in a new subject.
- Remote Work: Professionals can explore far flung task possibilities, offering the capability to work from everywhere and gain a higher work life balance.

RETIREES

Supplement Retirement Income: Retirees can earn extra earnings to complement their pensions or savings, improving their monetary protection.

- Staying Engaged: Online paintings can offer retirees with a experience of purpose and engagement, maintaining their minds lively and linked to the broader world.

- Flexible Hours: The flexibility of online work permits retirees to set their very own tempo and work in keeping with their preferences.

ASPIRING ENTREPRENEURS

- Low Start Up Costs: Online groups often require minimum preliminary funding, making it on hand for aspiring marketers to begin their ventures.
- Global Market Access: Entrepreneurs can reach a international target market, increasing their market ability beyond geographical boundaries.
- Scalability: Online companies provide the potential for rapid growth and scalability, permitting marketers to build and make bigger their establishments.

CREATIVE INDIVIDUALS

- Monetizing Creativity: Artists, writers, musicians, and different creatives can monetize their competencies through diverse on-line structures and possibilities.
- Building an Audience: The internet presents a platform for innovative people to showcase their paintings, construct a following, and interact with their audience.
- Collaborative Opportunities: Creatives can collaborate with manufacturers, different artists, and influencers to create unique and profitable projects.

ANYONE SEEKING FLEXIBILITY

Remote Work: Individuals seeking the freedom to paintings from everywhere can locate faraway task possibilities and freelance gigs on-line.

- Customization Work Hours: Online paintings permits individuals to set their own schedules, providing a level of flexible that traditional jobs often do now not offer.
- Personalized Career Paths: The internet permits individuals to carve out particular profession paths tailor-made to their capabilities, interests, and way of life choices.

CHAPTER 1: UNDERSTANDING THE ONLINE MARKETPLACE

THE GROWTH OF ONLINE BUSINESS

Benefits and Challenges

While the capability to make cash on-line is vast, it's essential to method this adventure with a balanced understanding of both the blessings and the challenges.

BENEFITS OF MAKING MONEY ONLINE

1. Flexibility and Freedom

- Work from Anywhere: The internet allows you to work from any location, whether or not it's your home, a cafe, or while travelling.
- Set Your Own Hours: You can pick whilst to paintings, making it easier to balance private commitments and paintings.

2. Low Start Up Costs
- Minimal Initial Investment: Many online business models require little to no startup capital, making them handy to a extensive audience.
- Affordable Tools and Resources: There are severa free and affordable equipment to be had to help you get began, from website builders to advertising and marketing software.

3. Scalability
- Growth Potential: Online agencies can scale speedy, accomplishing a international audience without the constraints of a bodily vicinity.
- Automated Processes: Automation gear can take care of repetitive responsibilities, permitting you to recognition on increase and strategy.

4. Diverse Opportunities
- Variety of Income Streams: From freelancing to e commerce, there are numerous methods to make money on-line, allowing you to diversify your income.
- Adaptability: You can pivot or add new sales streams as marketplace developments and private pursuits exchange.

5. Skill Development
- Learning Opportunities: Engaging in on-line work will let you broaden treasured talents in areas like virtual advertising, content material advent, and customer service.
- Professional Growth: Building a web enterprise or freelance career can decorate your resume and open up new profession possibilities.

6. Financial Independence
- Control Over Earnings: Your earnings capacity is often without delay tied for your efforts and creativity, supplying the opportunity of unlimited earning capability.
- Multiple Income Streams: Diversifying your online income can provide economic stability and security.

CHALLENGES OF MAKING MONEY ONLINE

1. Initial Learning Curve
- Technical Skills: Understanding and the usage of digital tools and systems can be challenging for novices.
- Marketing Knowledge: Successfully selling your on line business or services calls for a terrific grasp of virtual advertising and marketing strategies.

2. Competition
- Saturated Markets: Many on line niches are especially competitive, making it tough to stand out and entice clients.
- Continuous Innovation: Staying beforehand of the opposition requires regular innovation and version to new developments.

3. Income Variability
- Inconsistent Earnings: Online profits can be unpredictable, in particular inside the early tiers of your mission.
- Seasonal Fluctuations: Certain on line agencies may revel in seasonal variations in profits.

4. Time Management
- Self Discipline: Working online calls for strong self discipline and time control abilities to keep away from distractions and keep productiveness.

- Work Life Balance: It can be challenging to split work from private lifestyles whilst operating from home.

5. Building Trust and Credibility
- Establishing Authority: Gaining the believe of your audience or customers takes time and steady effort.
- Maintaining Reputation: Online reputations are vital and may be effortlessly broken by terrible evaluations or negative customer service.

ESSENTIAL SKILLS FOR SUCCESS

Succeeding in the on line market calls for a numerous set of abilities. Whether you're freelancing, running an e commerce shop, or developing content material, studying the subsequent abilities will considerably decorate your probabilities of achievement.

1. Digital Literacy
- Understanding Technology: Basic pc abilities, internet navigation, and familiarity with various on line gear and platforms.
- Online Security: Knowledge of cyber security practices to guard your statistics and privateness.

2. Communication Skills
- Written Communication: Proficiency in writing clear, concise, and tasty content material for emails, blogs, social media, and client inquiries.
- Verbal Communication: Effective talking talents for virtual meetings, webinars, and customer service.

3. Marketing and Sales
- Digital Marketing: Understanding search engine marketing, social media advertising, e mail advertising, and

payper click advertising to promote your commercial enterprise.
- Sales Techniques: Ability to promote services or products, negotiate offers, and near income effectively.

4. Time Management
- Prioritization: Identifying and specializing in duties that provide the maximum value.
- Productivity Tools: Using calendars, to do lists, and project control software program to organize and track your work.

5. Financial Management
- Budgeting: Managing costs, placing financial desires, and creating a price range.
- Accounting: Basic information of bookkeeping, invoicing, and tax obligations.

6. Content Creation

- Writing: Crafting compelling articles, blog posts, and social media updates.
- Graphic Design: Creating visually appealing photos, pictures, and info graphics the usage of tools like Canva or Adobe Creative Suite.
- Video Production: Recording, modifying, and producing high quality movies for YouTube, social media, or on line guides.

CHAPTER 2: FREELANCING

IDENTIFYING MARKETABLE SKILLS

POPULAR FREELANCING PLATFORMS (E.G., UP WORK, FIVERR)

Popular Freelancing Platforms

Freelancing has grow to be a popular manner to make cash on line, supplying flexibility and the possibility to work on diverse tasks.

1. Up work
- Overview: Up work is considered one of the largest freelancing systems, offering a wide range of activity classes including writing, graphic design, programming, and advertising and marketing.

Features:
- Job Posting and Bidding: Clients publish jobs and freelancers bid on them, offering their rates and timelines.
- Profiles and Portfolios: Freelancers can create targeted profiles showcasing their skills, revel in, and previous paintings.
- Payment Protection: Up work provides price protection for hourly and fixed price projects, making sure freelancers get paid for his or her paintings.
- Best For: Professionals seeking out long term projects and higher paying customers.

2. Fiver
- Overview: Fiver is understood for its "gig" version, in which freelancers offer specific offerings at beginning costs as low as $five.

Features:

- Gig Listings: Freelancers create service listings (gigs) detailing what they provide and set their own charges.
- Packages: Freelancers can offer special applications with varying tiers of provider and pricing.
- Buyer Requests: Clients can put up unique task requests, and freelancers can reply with their offers.
- Best For: Freelancers presenting short, well defined services and those looking to construct a portfolio.

3. Freelancer

Overview: Freelancer.Com offers a giant market for freelancers and clients throughout severa industries.

Features:

- Contests: Clients can preserve contests for freelancers to post their work, with the great submission triumphing the prize.

- Project Bidding: Freelancers bid on tasks, and customers pick the fine healthy based on proposals.
- Milestone Payments: Payments are made via milestones, ensuring freelancers receives a commission as challenge tiers are completed.
- Best For: Freelancers seeking a lot of assignment types, including contests and traditional undertaking bids.

4. Top tal

Overview: Top tal is an one of a kind community of top freelancers in fields like software improvement, design, and finance.

Features:

- Screening Process: Top tal has a rigorous screening procedure to make sure handiest the pinnacle 3% of freelancers are typical.

- High Quality Clients: Freelancers on Top tal paintings with top groups and startups.
- Matching Service: Top tal fits freelancers with customers primarily based on undertaking requirements and freelancer expertise.
- Best For: Highly professional experts in search of high quality, well paying tasks.

5. Guru

- Overview: Guru connects freelancers with customers searching out specific talents in areas along with writing, design, IT, and commercial enterprise consulting.

Features:

- Work Rooms: Collaborative areas wherein groups can work on projects together.

- Payment Options: Multiple payment options, which include hourly, milestone based, and recurring payments.
- Safe Pay: An escrow carrier that guarantees freelancers are paid for his or her paintings.
- Best For: Freelancers looking for a bendy and collaborative platform with diverse fee alternatives.

6. People Per Hour
- Overview: People Per Hour specializes in connecting freelancers with customers for project based work.
- Features:
- Houries: Prepackaged services presented via freelancers at a hard and fast rate.
- Proposal System: Freelancers submit proposals for posted jobs, detailing their technique and pricing.

- Work Stream: A tool that manages communications, challenge management, and bills in one vicinity.
- Best For: Freelancers providing specific services and those searching out both short term and long term projects.

7. Flex Jobs

- Overview: Flex Jobs makes a speciality of far flung, part time, and freelance job listings.

Features:

- Curated Listings: All process postings are screened for legitimacy, making sure a scam free enjoy.
- Career Resources: Offers assets along with resume opinions, profession education, and abilities checking out.
- Membership Model: Requires a paid membership to get right of entry to task listings.

Best For: Freelancers looking for faraway, flexible, and valid job possibilities.

BUILDING A PORTFOLIO

A strong portfolio is vital for freelancers to show off their talents, revel in, and the satisfactory in their paintings. It serves as a visible resume that can attract capability clients and set you apart from the competition.

1. Determine Your Niche

- Identify Your Skills: List your center competencies and the services you provide.
- Target Audience: Define your best patron and the enterprise you want to work in.
- Specialization: Consider specializing in a particular niche to highlight your know-how and attract focused clients.

2. Choose a Platform
- Personal Website: Creating a personal website the use of platforms like WordPress, Wix, or Square space lets in complete customization and control over your portfolio.
- Freelancing Platforms: Utilize builtin portfolio capabilities on platforms like Up work, Fiver, and Freelancer.

3. Showcase Your Best Work
- Quality Over Quantity: Select your great and most applicable paintings samples. It's better to have some high quality pieces than a massive quantity of average ones.
- Variety: Include a number paintings that demonstrates your versatility and ability to address one-of-a-kind kinds of initiatives.
- Recent Work: Make certain your portfolio includes current initiatives to

expose that you are actively operating to your subject.

4. Provide Context
- Project Descriptions: Include quick descriptions of each undertaking, outlining the purchaser's necessities, your technique, and the consequences.
- Role and Contributions: Clearly country your role inside the assignment and the precise contributions you made.
- Results and Impact: Whenever possible, spotlight measurable results, including increased visitors, sales, or consumer engagement.

5. Include Testimonials
- Client Feedback: Request testimonials from satisfied clients to feature credibility for your portfolio.
- Highlight Positive Experiences: Include quotes that especially mention the exceptional of your work, your

professionalism, and the effect you made on their initiatives.

6. Keep It Organized

- Categories: Organize your work into classes or sections, making it smooth for potential clients to navigate and discover applicable samples.
- Tags and Filters: Use tags or filters to assist site visitors speedy locate the sort of paintings they may be inquisitive about.

7. Highlight Your Process

- Step by Step Breakdown: Provide insights into your creative or problem solving technique, displaying the way you technique and execute tasks.
- Behind the Scenes: Include sketches, drafts, or prototypes to illustrate your workflow and interest to element.

8. Personalize Your Portfolio
- About Me Section: Include a short biography that highlights your background, abilities, and what makes you precise.
- Professional Head shot: Add a expert photograph to create a personal connection with potential customers.
- Contact Information: Make it smooth for clients to reach you by means of consisting of your touch info and hyperlinks for your social media profiles.

9. Update Regularly
- New Projects: Continuously upload new paintings samples to maintain your portfolio sparkling and up to date.
- Remove Outdated Work: Periodically evaluation and cast off older or less relevant initiatives to hold a high popular.

- Refresh Design: Update the layout and format of your portfolio to keep it present day and visually attractive.

10. Promote Your Portfolio

- Social Media: Share your portfolio on social media systems to increase visibility and attract potential clients.
- Networking: Include a hyperlink for your portfolio for your electronic mail signature, commercial enterprise playing cards, and any professional networking profiles.
- SEO: Optimize your portfolio for search engines like google and yahoo to increase its discover ability.

SETTING COMPETITIVE RATES

Determining how tons to rate in your services is a vital thing of freelancing. Setting aggressive prices involves balancing the need to attract clients with making sure that your income are sustainable and reflective of your abilities and enjoy.

1. Understand the Market

- Research Industry Standards: Investigate the everyday costs on your services inside your industry. Websites like Glass door, Pay scale, and freelancing structures can provide treasured insights.
- Analyze Competitors: Look at what different freelancers with comparable abilities and experience are charging. Check their profiles on platforms like Up work, Fiver, and LinkedIn.

2. Consider Your Experience and Skills

Entry Level: If you're simply beginning, you would possibly want to set decrease charges to attract preliminary customers and build your portfolio.

Intermediate: With some years of enjoy and a solid portfolio, you can price mid range rates.

Expert: If you have giant revel in, specialized competencies, or a sturdy popularity, you could command higher costs.

3. Calculate Your Costs

- Business Expenses: Include fees like software, system, workplace supplies, and advertising and marketing.
- Living Expenses: Calculate your non-public dwelling expenses to make sure your rates cover your monetary desires.
- Taxes and Benefits: Remember to aspect in taxes, coverage, retirement savings, and other benefits normally protected by way of conventional employment.

4. Determine Your Rate Structure

- Hourly Rates: Common for ongoing or less defined initiatives. Set an hourly charge based for your preferred annual income divided through the variety of billable hours.
- Project Based Rates: Suitable for well defined initiatives. Estimate the overall hours wished and multiply through your hourly fee, adding a buffer for sudden changes.
- Retainer Fees: Regular, habitual payments for ongoing work. Clients pay a fixed amount month-to-month for a fixed range of hours or deliverable.
- Value Based Pricing: Charge based on the price you provide to the patron, rather than the time spent. This may be more beneficial but calls for a clean demonstration of your effect.

5. Set a Baseline Rate

- Minimum Acceptable Rate: Calculate the lowest price you could accept to fulfill your financial needs and cowl your charges. This is your baseline, and you should purpose to rate above it on every occasion viable.
- Desired Rate: Determine your ideal fee that reflects your skills, revel in, and market situations.

6. Adjust for Complexity and Urgency

- Complex Projects: Charge better prices for tasks that require specialized competencies, advanced strategies, or sizable research.
- Tight Deadlines: Apply a premium for urgent initiatives that require short turnaround times.

7. Communicate Value
- Highlight Benefits: Emphasize the cost you bring to clients, including extended income, advanced performance, or stronger logo image.
- Case Studies and Testimonials: Use beyond successes and purchaser testimonials to justify your fees.

FINDING AND RETAINING CLIENTS

Successfully finding and maintaining clients is important for building a sustainable and thriving freelance career. This segment outlines powerful strategies to draw new clients and maintain robust relationships with current ones.

FINDING CLIENTS

1. Leverage Freelance Platforms
- Create Comprehensive Profiles: Use platforms like Up work, Fiverr, Freelancer, and Top tal to reach capability customers. Make positive

your profile is precise, showcasing your abilties, revel in, and portfolio.

- Bid on Projects: Actively look for and bid on tasks that fit your knowledge. Tailor each idea to cope with the particular wishes of the customer.

2. Network Professionally

- Attend Industry Events: Participate in meetings, webinars, and networking events to satisfy capability customers and industry peers.

- Join Professional Associations: Become a member of relevant professional businesses and associations to get admission to special process boards and networking opportunities.

- Online Networking: Use LinkedIn to connect with industry professionals, be part of relevant businesses, and engage in discussions to boom your visibility.

3. Utilize Social Media
- Showcase Your Work: Use systems like Instagram, Twitter, and Facebook to share your portfolio, success memories, and industry insights.
- Engage with Your Audience: Interact together with your fans via responding to comments, sharing valuable content material, and collaborating in relevant conversations.

4. Create a Professional Website
- Showcase Your Services: Clearly define the services you provide, along with examples of your paintings, purchaser testimonials, and a compelling "About Me" phase.
- Search engine marketing Optimization: Optimize your website for search engines like google and yahoo to draw natural site visitors. Use applicable keywords, create treasured content

material, and make certain your website online is mobile friendly.

5. Offer Free Value
- Free Workshops or Webinars: Host free on-line sessions to demonstrate your expertise and entice capacity customers.
- Guest Blogging: Write visitor posts for legit enterprise blogs to growth your visibility and establish your authority.

6. Ask for Referrals
- Satisfied Clients: Request referrals from glad customers. A positive advice may be a powerful tool for attracting new commercial enterprise.
- Referral Incentives: Offer discounts or different incentives for clients who refer new commercial enterprise to you.

RETAINING CLIENTS

1. Deliver High Quality Work
- Exceed Expectations: Consistently deliver work that meets or exceeds

customer expectancies in phrases of satisfactory and timeliness.

- Attention to Detail: Pay near attention to client briefs and necessities to make sure accuracy and relevance in your paintings.

2. Communicate Effectively

- Regular Updates: Keep customers informed approximately the progress in their initiatives through ordinary updates.
- Prompt Responses: Respond to customer inquiries and messages promptly to expose your commitment and reliability.

3. Build Strong Relationships

- Personal Touch: Get to understand your customers and their corporations. Show proper hobby of their success.
- Professionalism: Maintain a excessive stage of professionalism in all

interactions, together with being respectful, courteous, and punctual.

4. Be Flexible and Adaptable

- Accommodate Changes: Be willing to house reasonable adjustments and revisions to make certain patron pride.
- Adapt to Feedback: Actively seek and reply to patron comments to improve your offerings and meet their desires higher.

5. Offer Additional Services

- Up sell and Cross Sell: Identify possibilities to offer additional services that supplement your present paintings.
- Package Deals: Create carrier applications that provide clients greater price and convenience, encouraging them to choose you for a couple of wishes.

6. Maintain Consistent Quality
- Ongoing Learning: Continuously update your abilities and expertise to offer the cutting-edge and first-class solutions to your clients.
- Quality Control: Implement a sturdy excellent manipulate method to make certain the consistency and excellence of your paintings.

7. Create Long Term Contracts
- Retainer Agreements: Offer retainer agreements for ongoing offerings, imparting balance for both you and your clients.
- Loyalty Discounts: Provide loyalty reductions or special fees for long term clients to encourage continued collaboration.

8. Show Appreciation

- Thank You Notes: Send personalized thank you notes or emails to explicit your gratitude for their commercial enterprise.
- Client Gifts: Occasionally ship small tokens of appreciation to show customers they're valued.

CHAPTER 3: BLOGGING AND CONTENT CREATION

CHOOSING A NICHE

CREATING ENGAGING CONTENT

Creating attractive content material is crucial for attracting and maintaining an target audience, whether or not you are a freelancer, business owner, or content writer. Engaging content captures interest, fosters interplay, and encourages sharing.

1. Understand Your Audience
- Research Your Audience: Use gear like Google Analytic, social media insights, and surveys to collect statistics approximately your target audience's demographics, choices, and behaviors.
- Create Buyer Personas: Develop certain profiles of your perfect target audience

segments, including their goals, demanding situations, and interests.

2. Craft Compelling Headlines
- Attention Grabbing: Write headlines that capture interest and spark curiosity.
- Clear and Concise: Ensure your headlines are clear and produce the principle concept of the content.
- Use Numbers and Power Words: Incorporate numbers, lists, and powerful phrases to make headlines more attractive (e.G., "10 Tips for...", "Ultimate Guide to...").

3. Use Visual Elements
- High Quality Images: Include relevant, high quality pictures to interrupt up textual content and illustrate your points.
- Info graphics: Use info graphics to offer records and complicated data in an easy tounder stand format.

- Videos: Incorporate movies to decorate engagement, provide an explanation for concepts, or exhibit products.

4. Tell a Story
- Narrative Structure: Use a clean starting, middle, and stop to structure your content.
- Personal Touch: Share non-public studies or anecdotes to make your content material relatable and proper.
- Emotional Connection: Tap into emotions by addressing your target audience's hopes, fears, and aspirations.

5. Provide Value
- Educational Content: Offer recommendations, how tos, and tutorials that remedy problems or educate new skills.
- Informative Content: Share enterprise news, studies, and insights that hold your audience knowledgeable.

- Entertaining Content: Use humor, interesting information, or enticing tales to entertain your target audience while handing over your message.

6. Make It Interactive

- Ask Questions: Encourage your target audience to engage through asking questions and prompting discussions.
- Polls and Surveys: Use polls and surveys to collect opinions and insights, making your target market sense involved.
- Interactive Tools: Incorporate interactive tools like quizzes, calculators, and interactive info graphics.

7. Optimize for SEO

- Keyword Research: Use tools like Google Keyword Planner and Ah refs to find relevant key phrases and terms.
- On Page SEO: Optimize your content material with relevant key phrases

within the title, headers, meta descriptions, and for the duration of the content.
- Link Building: Include internal and external hyperlinks to offer additional value and enhance SEO.

8. Maintain Readability
- Short Paragraphs: Use brief paragraphs and sentences to make your content material easy to read.
- Subheadings: Break up your content with descriptive subheadings to guide the reader.
- Bullet Points and Lists: Use bullet factors and numbered lists to offer information really and concisely.

9. Engage on Social Media
- Shareable Content: Create content that is easy to share on social media structures.

- Social Media Optimization: Optimize your content for distinct social media platforms by means of the use of the proper codes, lengths, and hashtags.
- Engage with Comments: Respond to feedback and have interaction together with your target audience to build a community round your content.

10. Monitor and Adapt

- Analytic and Feedback: Use analytic tools to music engagement metrics like views, stocks, remarks, and time spent at the content.
- Iterative Improvement: Continuously refine your content method primarily based on remarks and overall performance records.
- Stay Updated: Keep up with developments and changes to your enterprise to make sure your content remains applicable and clean.

Monetization Strategies (Ads, Sponsored Posts, Affiliate Marketing)

MONETIZATION STRATEGIES

Monetizing your on line content material is critical for turning your efforts into revenue. Whether you create blogs, movies, podcasts, or social media content material,

1. Advertising

- Display Ads: Place banner ads or text ads for your internet site or blog. Common advert networks include Google Ad Sense, Media.Internet, and Ad Thrive.
- Video Ads: Monetize YouTube motion pictures with ads via the YouTube Partner Program. Consider integrating mid roll and overlay commercials.

2. Sponsored Posts and Brand Collaborations

- Sponsored Content: Collaborate with manufacturers to create backed posts,

critiques, or endorsements. Ensure transparency through disclosing sponsored content in your audience.
- Brand Ambassadorships: Represent a logo thru ongoing partnerships, selling their products or services to your content material.
- Influencer Campaigns: Participate in influencer advertising and marketing campaigns where manufacturers pay you to sell their services or products.

3. Affiliate Marketing
- Affiliate Programs: Join affiliate packages relevant in your niche (e.G., Amazon Associates, Share A Sale, Commission Junction). Earn commissions by selling products or services via precise associate links.
- Product Reviews: Write or create content that includes associate hyperlinks to merchandise you endorse.

Disclose affiliate relationships to maintain transparency.

4. Membership or Subscription Models

- Membership Sites: Create unique content or groups handy to paying individuals. Platforms like Patreon and Sub stack assist club fashions.
- Subscription Services: Offer sub scription based get right of entry to to top class content material, gear, or offerings. Platforms like Only Fans and YouTube Channel Memberships assist subscription models.

6. Crowdfunding and Donations

- Crowdfunding: Use systems like Kick starter or Indie gogo to fund innovative tasks or product launches.
- Donations: Accept donations or guidelines from your target market thru systems like PayPal, Buy Me a Coffee, or Patreon.

7. Events and Webinars

Virtual Events: Host webinars, workshops, or digital meetings, charging registration fees or sponsorship.

Live Streaming: Monetize stay streams via suggestions, donations, or sponsorship on structures like Twitch or Facebook Live.

8. Licensing and Syndication

Content Licensing: License your content (e.G., photos, articles, movies) to be used through different creators, publishers, or media stores.

Syndication: Distribute your content material to multiple platforms or guides for a fee, attaining broader audiences.

9. Sponsored Ads on Social Media

Paid Social Media Posts: Promote sponsored posts on systems like Instagram, Facebook, Twitter, and LinkedIn, focused on unique demographics or pastimes.

10. Consulting and Coaching
- Expertise Monetization: Offer consulting or training services based totally on your enterprise know-how or specialized information.

CHOOSING THE RIGHT STRATEGY

- Diversification: Consider combining a couple of monetization strategies to maximize sales streams and mitigate risks.
- Audience Alignment: Choose strategies that align with your audience's alternatives and needs to preserve engagement and consider.
- Experimentation: Test different strategies to look what works quality to your content format, niche, and target market demographics.

BUILDING AND GROWING AN AUDIENCE

Building and developing an audience is fundamental to the achievement of any on line endeavor, whether you are a blogger, content author, freelancer, or commercial enterprise proprietor.

1. Define Your Niche and Audience
- Identify Your Niche: Determine your specific place of understanding or the subjects you need to consciousness on.
- Target Audience: Develop distinctive consumer personas to apprehend your target audience's demographics, pastimes, ache points, and alternatives.

2. Create High Quality Content
- Content Strategy: Plan your content round your niche and target audience alternatives.
- Quality Over Quantity: Focus on developing treasured, applicable, and

well researched content that addresses your target audience's wishes.
- Consistency: Establish a everyday posting agenda to preserve your audience engaged and returning for more.

3. Optimize for Search Engines (SEO)
- Keyword Research: Use gear like Google Keyword Planner, SEMrush, or Ahrefs to find applicable key phrases and subjects.
- On Page Optimization: Optimize your content material with key phrases in titles, headers, meta descriptions, and for the duration of the text.
- Quality Back links: Build back links from reliable websites to enhance your search engine rating.

4. Leverage Social Media
- Platform Selection: Choose social media platforms wherein your target

audience is most lively (e.G., Instagram, Facebook, Twitter, LinkedIn).
- Engagement: Actively interact with your target market through feedback, messages, and sharing precious content.
- Visual Content: Use high quality pics, movies, info graphics, and stories to boom engagement.

5. Build an Email List
- Lead Magnet: Offer a valuable useful resource (e.G., e-book, tick list, webinar) in trade for email subscriptions.
- Email Campaigns: Send everyday newsletters with updates, one of a kind content, promotions, and personalized messages.
- Segmentation: Segment your e-mail listing based on interests or conduct to deliver targeted content and offers.

6. Collaborate and Network

- Guest Blogging: Write guest posts for famous blogs to your niche to attain new audiences and construct one-way links.
- Influencer Collaborations: Partner with influencers or enterprise professionals to reach their fans and make bigger your attain.
- Networking: Attend industry activities, webinars, and on-line communities to hook up with like minded experts and capacity collaborators.

CHAPTER FOUR: AFFILIATE MARKETING

HOW AFFILIATE MARKETING WORKS

CHOOSING THE RIGHT PROGRAMS

Choosing the proper programs and techniques to build and develop your audience relies upon in your desires, target audience demographics, and the form of content you create.

1. Content Creation Platforms

- Blogging Platforms: Use systems like WordPress, Medium, or Ghost to submit articles and reach a huge target market interested by written content material.
- Video Platforms: YouTube and Vimeo are perfect for creating and sharing video content material, tutorials, vlogs, and greater.

- Podcasting Platforms: Platforms like Apple Podcasts, Spotify, and Google Podcasts are terrific for achieving audiences through audio content material.

2. Social Media Platforms

- Instagram: Ideal for visible content material, photography, style, way of life, and reaching younger demographics.
- Facebook: Versatile for numerous content material sorts, from textual content posts to films and stay streaming, appropriate for vast audiences.
- Twitter: Best for short updates, news, traits, and tasty in real time conversations.
- LinkedIn: Perfect for expert networking, B2B content, industry insights, and notion leadership.

Pinterest: Great for visible content material, DIY projects, recipes, fashion, and home decor.

3. Email Marketing Platforms
- Mail chimp: Offers easy touse templates, automation, and analytics for e-mail campaigns and newsletters.
- Convert Kit: Designed for creators with customization forms, touchdown pages, and automatic e mail sequences.
- Hub Spot: Provides comprehensive marketing automation, CRM integration, and superior analytic for larger scale operations.

4. Search engine optimization Tools
- Google Analytics: Essential for tracking website site visitors, person behavior, and conversion charges.
- Ahrefs: Useful for keyword studies, back-link evaluation, and search engine optimization audits.

SEM rush: Offers aggressive evaluation, key-word tracking, and search engine optimization suggestions.

5. Advertising and Paid Promotion
- Google Ads: Ideal for concentrated on precise keywords and demographics thru seek and show advertisements.
- Facebook Ads: Offers distinct audience targeting alternatives primarily based on pastimes, behaviors, and demographics.
- Instagram Ads: Integrates seamlessly with Facebook Ads Manager, specializing in visual content material and cell customers.
- LinkedIn Ads: Perfect for B2B advertising and marketing, targeting experts primarily based on task title, industry, and company length.

CREATING AND PROMOTING CONTENT

Creating and promoting content material efficaciously is crucial for reaching and engaging your audience.

1. Content Creation

Define Your Audience and Goals

- Audience Persona: Understand your target audience's demographics, pastimes, ache points, and preferences.
- Content Goals: Determine whether you goal to teach, entertain, inspire, or persuade your audience.

CONTENT TYPES

- Blog Posts: Informative articles, how to courses, listicles, and industry insights.
- Videos: Tutorials, vlogs, product critiques, interviews, and behind the scenes content.
- Info graphics: Visual representations of statistics, statistics, or tactics.
- Podcasts: Audio episodes protecting subjects of interest in your target market.

CONTENT CREATION TIPS

- Quality Over Quantity: Focus on generating high quality content material that offers price for your target audience.
- Storytelling: Incorporate storytelling strategies to engage and hook up with your target audience emotionally.
- SEO Optimization: Use applicable key phrases, meta descriptions, and tags to improve visibility on search engines like google.
- Visual Appeal: Include high quality photographs, pix, or films to decorate engagement.

2. Content Promotion

Social Media Promotion

- Platform Selection: Choose social media systems in which your audience is most energetic (e.G., Instagram, Facebook, LinkedIn, Twitter).

- Scheduled Posts: Use scheduling equipment like Buffer or Hoot suite to plan and automate content material distribution.
- Engagement: Actively have interaction with your target market thru remarks, shares, and direct messages.
- Paid Advertising: Boost posts or run centered advert campaigns to attain a broader target market.

EMAIL MARKETING

Build an Email List: Offer incentives like ebooks, webinars, or discounts to encourage sign ups.

- Newsletter Campaigns: Send normal newsletters with curated content material, updates, and one-of-a-kind offers.
- Segmentation: Segment your electronic mail list primarily based on interests or behaviors to personalize content and improve engagement.

- Search engine optimization Strategies
- Keyword Research: Use tools like Google Keyword Planner, SEMrush, or Ahrefs to locate applicable key phrases.
- On Page SEO: Optimize titles, headers, meta descriptions, and content with centered key phrases.
- Back links: Build quality inbound links from official websites to improve search engine scores.

COLLABORATIONS AND PARTNERSHIPS

- Guest Blogging: Write visitor posts for popular blogs on your industry to reach new audiences.
- Influencer Partnerships: Collaborate with influencers or industry experts to sell your content to their fans.
- Cross Promotion: Partner with complementary manufacturers or

organizations to cocreate and percentage content material.

CONTENT DISTRIBUTION CHANNELS

- Content Aggregators: Submit content to systems like Reddit, Medium, or Flip board to reach broader audiences.
- Forums and Communities: Participate in relevant boards or on-line groups to share expertise and promote content.

Content Syndication: Distribute content via syndication structures or partnerships with media stores.

3. Analyze and Optimize

Analytics Tools

- Google Analytics: Track website site visitors, consumer behavior, and conversions to apprehend content material overall performance.
- Social Media Insights: Use platform specific analytic to measure engagement, attain, and audience demographics.

- A/B Testing: Experiment with one-of-a-kind content codes, headlines, or visuals to optimize overall performance.

TRACKING AND ANALYZING PERFORMANCE

Tracking and analyzing overall performance is crucial to know-how how well your content material and advertising efforts are acting.

1. Define Key Performance Indicators (KPIs)

TRAFFIC METRICS

- Website Traffic: Measure total visits, precise traffic, and web page views the usage of tools like Google Analytics.
- Traffic Sources: Identify where your site visitors is coming from (e.G., organic seek, social media, referrals).
- Conversion Rate: Track the proportion of site visitors who whole desired movements (e.G., sign ups, purchases).

ENGAGEMENT METRICS

- Bounce Rate: Measure the share of visitors who leave your web page after viewing most effective one web page.
- Average Session Duration: Determine how lengthy site visitors spend on your web site or specific pages.

Pages in line with Session: Track the average range of pages traffic view at some stage in a consultation.

CONTENT PERFORMANCE METRICS

- Most Popular Content: Identify which pages or posts acquire the maximum visits and engagement.
- Top Performing Keywords: Monitor key phrases that pressure traffic and conversions via SEO efforts.
- Social Shares and Comments: Measure engagement on social media platforms and blog feedback.

2. Tools for Tracking Performance

Website Analytics

- Google Analytics: Provides precise insights into internet site site visitors, consumer behavior, and conversion metrics.
- Hot jar: Offers heat maps, consultation recordings, and user feedback to apprehend tourist conduct.
- Adobe Analytics: Advanced analytics platform for targeted purchaser journey evaluation and reporting.
- Social Media Analytics
- Facebook Insights: Provides statistics on web page likes, attain, engagement, and demographics.
- Twitter Analytics: Offers metrics on tweets, impressions, engagements, and follower boom.

- LinkedIn Analytics: Tracks web page perspectives, engagement, and follower demographics.
- Email Marketing Analytics
- Mail chimp: Tracks email open fees, click through rates, subscriber boom, and campaign overall performance.
- ConvertKit: Provides insights into electronic mail subscriber behavior, segmentation, and automation performance.

3. Setting Up Performance Tracking

Install Tracking Codes

- Google Analytics: Install the monitoring code on your website to start gathering records.
- Social Media Pixels: Set up pixels (e.G., Facebook Pixel) to music conversions and target audience conduct on social platforms.

CREATE CUSTOM DASHBOARDS AND REPORTS

- Google Data Studio: Build customizable dashboards to visualize and analyze data from multiple sources.
- Microsoft Power BI: Analyze and proportion interactive reviews with facts from various resources for complete insights.

4. Analyzing Performance

Regular Monitoring and Reporting

- Set Reporting Intervals: Schedule normal reviews of analytics facts (e.G., weekly, monthly) to track development and perceive tendencies.
- Compare Performance Over Time: Analyze adjustments in metrics and performance tendencies to evaluate the effectiveness of your techniques.
- Identify Opportunities and Challenges: Use insights to optimize content material,

marketing campaigns, and target audience engagement strategies.

5. Optimization Strategies

Optimize Content and search engine optimization

- Content Updates: Refresh and optimize under performing content material with up to date facts and advanced search engine optimization.
- Search engine optimization Adjustments: Refine keyword approach primarily based on overall performance statistics and modifications in seek engine algorithms.

SOCIAL MEDIA AND EMAIL CAMPAIGNS

- A/B Testing: Experiment with exclusive content codes, messaging, and visuals to improve engagement charges.
- Segmentation and Personalization: Tailor electronic mail content material

and social media campaigns based on target audience preferences and behaviors.

6. Continuous Improvement

FEEDBACK AND ITERATION

Audience Feedback: Gather insights from surveys, feedback, and social media interactions to refine content approach.

Benchmark Against Goals: Compare overall performance against predefined KPIs and alter strategies to gain goals.

MAXIMIZING EARNINGS

Maximizing earnings out of your on-line activities entails leveraging various strategies across monetization, target market growth, and optimization of your virtual presence.

1. Diversify Monetization Strategies

ADVERTISING REVENUE

Display Ads: Use structures like Google Ad Sense, Media.Net, or Ad Thrive to show commercials in your internet site or weblog.

Video Ads: Monetize YouTube movies thru the YouTube Partner Program or integrate advertisements into your video content.

Podcast Ads: Include sponsorship or commercials within your podcast episodes.

AFFILIATE MARKETING

- Join Programs: Partner with affiliate networks including Amazon Associates, Share A Sale, or Commission Junction to sell merchandise relevant for your target audience.
- Promotional Content: Create content (e.G., critiques, tutorials) with associate links and disclosures to earn commissions on income.

SPONSORED CONTENT AND BRAND COLLABORATIONS

- Sponsored Posts: Collaborate with manufacturers to create sponsored content material, product evaluations, or endorsements.
- Brand Ambassadorships: Establish ongoing partnerships with brands to sell their services or products.

DIRECT SALES OF PRODUCTS OR SERVICES

E commerce: Sell bodily products via structures like Shopify, Etsy, or Woo Commerce.

- Digital Products: Offer virtual items consisting of ebooks, publications, templates, or software program equipment on systems like Gumroad or Teachable.

- Services: Provide consulting, education, design, or freelance services primarily based on your knowledge.

SUBSCRIPTION MODELS AND MEMBERSHIP PROGRAMS

- Membership Sites: Offer unique content, network get entry to, or premium offerings via systems like Sub stack.
- Subscription Services: Provide ordinary get admission to to specialized content material or services, making sure steady sales streams.

2. Optimize Audience Growth and Engagement

Content Strategy

- Quality Content: Create treasured, high quality content material that resonates with your target market's pursuits and needs.
- Search engine optimization Optimization: Optimize content material

for search engines like google and yahoo to draw natural site visitors through relevant keywords and search engine marketing quality practices.

Consistency: Maintain a normal posting agenda to preserve your target audience engaged and returning for extra content.

AUDIENCE ENGAGEMENT

- Social Media Engagement: Actively have interaction along with your target audience on systems like Instagram, Facebook, Twitter, and LinkedIn via remarks, messages, and live periods.
- Email Marketing: Build and nurture an e mail list, turning in personalized content material and promotions to subscribers.
- Community Building: Foster a feel of network through boards, social businesses, or membership platforms,

encouraging member interplay and loyalty.

3. Analyze Performance and Optimize Strategies

Data Driven Decisions

- Analytics Tools: Use tools like Google Analytics, social media insights, and e mail advertising analytics to track overall performance metrics (e.G., site visitors, engagement, conversions).
- A/B Testing: Experiment with exceptional strategies, content material codes, and promotional approaches to identify what resonates nice with your target market.
- ROI Analysis: Evaluate the return on investment (ROI) for every monetization method and advertising marketing campaign to allocate sources effectively.

4. Strategic Partnerships and Collaborations

Influencer Collaborations

- Cross Promotion: Partner with influencers or complementary manufacturers to reach new audiences and extend your reach.
- Affiliate Partnerships: Collaborate with affiliates and referral companions to drive site visitors and sales thru collectively beneficial preparations.

5. Continuous Learning and Adaptation

STAY UPDATED

- Industry Trends: Keep abreast of enterprise tendencies, consumer behavior shifts, and rising technologies to adapt your strategies therefore.
- Feedback Mechanisms: Solicit feedback out of your audience and examine their choices and behaviors to refine your services and strategies.

CHAPTER 5: E COMMERCE AND DROP SHIPPING

SETTING UP AN ONLINE STORE (SHOPIFY, WOO COMMERCE)

Finding Profitable Products

Finding worthwhile products to promote on line involves strategic studies and understanding of market demand, competition, and patron alternatives.

1. Conduct Market Research

Identify Niche Markets

- Trending Niches: Research modern developments and emerging markets that align along with your interests or information.
- Unsaturated Niches: Explore area of interest markets with less opposition but sufficient demand.

Use Market Research Tools

- Google Trends: Analyze search trends to perceive rising pastimes and seasonal styles.
- Marketplaces: Explore structures like Amazon, eBay, or Etsy to gauge famous products and classes.
- Social Media: Monitor hashtags, businesses, and discussions on structures like Instagram, Facebook, and Reddit to pick out purchaser hobbies.

2. Evaluate Product Demand and Competition

Keyword Research

- search engine marketing Tools: Use equipment like Ahrefs, SEMrush, or Google Keyword Planner to investigate search volumes and opposition for applicable key phrases.

Longtail Keywords: Target particular phrases that suggest high purchase rationale and decrease competition.

COMPETITOR ANALYSIS

Top Sellers: Study topselling merchandise in your selected niche to recognize demand and pricing techniques.

Reviews and Feedback: Analyze patron reviews to identify product strengths, weaknesses, and opportunities for development.

3. Validate Profitability

Calculate Profit Margins

Cost Analysis: Determine product costs, which includes manufacturing, shipping, and overhead charges.

Pricing Strategy: Set competitive fees that allow for a appropriate profit margin even as considering market expectancies.

SUPPLIER AND SHIPPING COSTS

Supplier Research: Find reliable providers or manufacturers with competitive pricing and nice merchandise.

Shipping Options: Evaluate delivery expenses and logistics to ensure profitability and patron pride.

4. Consider Product Trends and Seasonality

Seasonal Products

Holiday Trends: Identify products with seasonal demand peaks at some point of holidays like Christmas, Valentine's Day, or Halloween.

Yearround Appeal: Choose products with steady demand during the yr to hold steady income.

5. Customer Feedback and Validation

Prototype Testing

Product Samples: Test product prototypes or samples with a focus institution or beta testers to collect remarks and identify capability enhancements.

Preorders: Gauge consumer hobby and call for through preorder campaigns or surveys earlier than making an investment in bulk inventory.

MANAGING SUPPLIERS AND INVENTORY

Managing suppliers and inventory efficiently is critical for maintaining clean operations and assembly customer call for.

1. Supplier Management

Finding Reliable Suppliers

Research and Vetting: Conduct thorough research to perceive reputable providers with a track record of first-class and reliability.

Supplier Networks: Utilize on line directories, change shows, and industry contacts to discover potential providers.

Samples and Trials: Request samples or conduct trials to assess product quality, reliability, and compatibility together with your business desires.

NEGOTIATING TERMS

- Price Negotiation: Negotiate aggressive pricing primarily based on bulk orders, longterm contracts, or exclusivity agreements.
- Payment Terms: Establish clean fee phrases, which include reductions for early payments or extent purchases.
- Contractual Agreements: Draft contracts outlining terms of service, great requirements, delivery schedules, and dispute resolution mechanisms.

Maintaining Relationships

Communication: Maintain open strains of conversation to cope with issues promptly and collaborate on upgrades.

Feedback: Provide positive remarks to providers to enhance product nice and provider transport.

Performance Evaluation: Regularly examine supplier performance based totally on metrics like satisfactory, transport instances, and responsiveness.

2. Inventory Management

Forecasting Demand

Historical Data: Analyze past income data and developments to forecast future call for accurately.

Market Trends: Monitor enterprise developments, seasonal versions, and consumer options to adjust stock stages as a consequence.

Demand Planning Tools: Use stock control software program or gear to automate call for forecasting and optimize inventory stages.

OPTIMIZING INVENTORY LEVELS

- Justin Time (JIT) Inventory: Maintain minimal stock degrees to lessen maintaining prices whilst assembly purchaser demand.
- Safety Stock: Maintain safety inventory tiers to mitigate risks of stockouts due to surprising call for spikes or supplier delays.
- ABC Analysis: Classify inventory gadgets based totally on their cost and prioritize control efforts for that reason (e.G., high value items require stricter manage).

INVENTORY TRACKING AND CONTROL

- Inventory Systems: Implement stock control software program to music inventory stages, orders, and replenishment cycles.

Barcoding/RFID: Use barcoding or RFID generation for correct stock tracking and real time visibility.

Cycle Counting: Conduct normal cycle counts or bodily inventories to reconcile real stock ranges with recorded facts.

3. Supply Chain Efficiency

Logistics and Fulfillment

- Shipping and Delivery: Optimize shipping methods and service relationships to reduce prices and make certain well timed transport.
- Warehouse Management: Streamline warehouse operations for efficient order picking, packing, and delivery.
- Reverse Logistics: Establish strategies for coping with returns, exchanges, and defective merchandise correctly.

CONTINUOUS IMPROVEMENT

- Performance Metrics: Monitor key overall performance signs (KPIs) together with inventory turnover, fill price, and dealer lead times to pick out areas for development.
- Process Optimization: Implement lean ideas and continuous development methodologies to streamline deliver chain operations.
- Supplier Collaboration: Collaborate with providers on procedure upgrades, price discounts, and sustainability tasks.

4. Risk Management

Supply Chain Risks

- Supplier Diversification: Diversify providers to reduce dependency risks and mitigate deliver chain disruptions.
- Contingency Planning: Develop contingency plans for handling disruptions which includes natural

failures, geopolitical occasions, or dealer bankruptcies.

- Compliance and Regulations: Stay informed about regulatory modifications and compliance requirements affecting stock control and supplier relationships.

MARKETING AND SALES STRATEGIES

Developing powerful advertising and marketing and sales strategies is critical for attracting customers, riding conversions, and developing your commercial enterprise on line.

1. Define Your Target Audience

Market Segmentation: Identify and section your audience based totally on demographics, pursuits, behaviors, and wishes.

Buyer Personas: Create unique profiles of your ideal clients to tailor your marketing messages and strategies efficiently.

2. Develop a Strong Brand Identity

- Brand Positioning: Clearly outline what sets your logo aside from competition and articulate your precise value proposition (UVP).
- Brand Messaging: Craft constant and compelling messaging that resonates with your target market throughout all channels.

3. Online Marketing Strategies

Content Marketing

Blog Posts and Articles: Create informative and engaging content that addresses purchaser ache factors, educates, or entertains.

Search engine marketing Optimization: Optimize content material for search engines like google and yahoo to attract natural traffic through relevant key phrases and meta tags.

Guest Blogging: Publish articles on reliable industry blogs to attain new audiences and build one-way links.

SOCIAL MEDIA MARKETING

Platform Selection: Choose social media platforms (e.G., Facebook, Instagram, LinkedIn, Twitter) where your audience is most active.

Content Strategy: Share precious content material, interact with fans, run contests, and leverage paid advertising to increase reach and engagement.

Influencer Collaborations: Partner with influencers to make bigger your logo's reach and credibility among st their fans.

EMAIL MARKETING

Build an Email List: Offer incentives (e.G., reductions, unfastened assets) to encourage signups and nurture leads.

Segmentation: Segment your e-mail list primarily based on demographics, behaviors, or buy records to personalize content and gives.

Automation: Use email automation tools to ship targeted campaigns, welcome sequences, and deserted cart reminders.

4. Paid Advertising

Google Ads: Run PPC (payperclick) campaigns to target unique key phrases and attain customers actively attempting to find your products or services.

Social Media Ads: Utilize Facebook Ads, Instagram Ads, LinkedIn Ads, etc., to target audiences based on demographics, interests, and behaviors.

Display Advertising: Place banner advertisements on relevant websites and platforms to increase emblem visibility and drive visitors.

5. Sales Strategies

Ecommerce Optimization

- User Experience (UX): Ensure your website is user friendly, mobile responsive, and optimized for immediate load times.
- Conversion Rate Optimization (CRO): Test and optimize your website's layout, format, and CTAs to improve conversion rates.
- Up selling and Cross selling: Recommend associated products or enhancements to growth average order price and patron pleasure.

CUSTOMER RELATIONSHIP MANAGEMENT (CRM)
- CRM Software: Use CRM equipment to tune patron interactions, manage leads, and personalize verbal exchange based on patron records.
- Lead Nurturing: Develop lead nurturing campaigns to guide possibilities via the

sales funnel with centered content and timely followups.

6. Analytics and Optimization

- Performance Tracking: Monitor key metrics (e.G., internet site visitors, conversion costs, ROI) the usage of analytics tools like Google Analytics, social media insights, and CRM dashboards.
- A/B Testing: Experiment with one of a kind techniques, advert creatives, and landing pages to identify what resonates best along with your audience.
- Continuous Improvement: Analyze facts insights to refine your advertising and sales strategies continuously, adapting to marketplace trends and purchaser feedback.

7. Customer Retention and Referral Programs
- Loyalty Programs: Reward repeat customers with extraordinary reductions, early get entry to to new products, or VIP perks.
- Referral Programs: Incentivize clients to refer buddies and own family via referral discounts, credit, or rewards.

8. Community Building and Engagement

Online Communities: Create or participate in boards, social corporations, or on line communities related to your industry or niche.

www.ingramcontent.com/pod-product-compliance
Lightning Source LLC
Chambersburg PA
CBHW071942210526
45479CB00002B/785